For Char

U

MW01064929

Adolfo

A Grief Revisited

Also by Adolfo Quezada

Compassionate Awareness

Radical Love

Sabbath Moments

Loving Yourself for God's Sake

Wholeness: The Legacy of Jesus

Walking with God

Goodbye, My Son, Hello

Rising from the Ashes

A Desert Place

Heart Peace

Of Mind and Spirit

Through the Darkness

The Teachings of Jesus

Transcending Illness

Old Soul, Young Spirit

A Grief Revisited

Weaving Loss into the Fabric of our Life

Adolfo Quezada

Contents

This book is dedicated to you who have suffered a major loss and are bereaved. May time be gentle with your wounded heart.

Foreword

In 1982, Adolfo's son, Roberto, died a tragic death. Three years later Adolfo wrote a book about his grief experience in the immediate aftermath of the death of his son entitled *Goodbye, My Son, Hello*. Adolfo asked me to write the foreword for that book. Now, thirty years later, we have a new book, which you are about to read, entitled, *A Grief Revisited: Weaving Loss into the Fabric of Our Life*. Once again, I have been asked to write the foreword for it.

In *A Grief Revisited* Adolfo and his family look back on more than three decades since Roberto's death to revisit and recount their grief experience as it impacted them individually and collectively.

In reading this manuscript, I discovered that Adolfo and I used similar means of responding to quite different traumas. His was to deal with a sudden, traumatic death with the tools at his disposal. As a counselor and journalist, and with his strong faith in God, and the support of others he was able to manage. My pathway was to offer a course on the Psychology of Death and Loss at the University of

Arizona to help me deal with several traumatic deaths that I needed to resolve. This is a universal lesson to us all – that we find ways to deal with grief that are unique to us, yet somehow similar to others. For Adolfo and for me, our professional skills came in handy. Here are the variables that make this process unique.

How one grieves depends on the kind of death we have to deal with. Was it natural, accidental, suicidal, or homicidal? Was our relationship to the deceased strong, dependent, unfinished, or ambivalent? How were we notified? What was our previous experience with death? Did we have support in grieving from others? What did our culture, religion, and family tell us that we were supposed to feel and do? Were there predisposing personal factors to who we are that would help or hinder our ability to grieve? Any current stresses in our life to complicate the situation? Dealing with a loss through death is like your fingerprint. No one has the same experience (finger print) that you do.

What is so marvelous about that very idea in this book is that Adolfo shows you how one person and one family copes in their own ways with the death of their son and brother. You will identify with some of these ways but probably not with all.

In my class on Death and Loss we would draw a line, as below:

Before a Death_____Death_____After the Death

Listen to Adolfo say, "If only I had spent more time with him," and Maria, Roberto's older sister, saying, "But I haven't made his cookies yet." We often judge ourselves with information about something we had no idea was about to happen. We use information after a death as though we should have anticipated the death before it happened. This is just one of a number of ways we can easily relate to Adolfo's story and admire his ability to work his way through the grief he has experienced.

You never stop grieving; it just becomes less prominent in your life. Put a little marker on the pages that speak to you. You will find some in there! Revisit them from time to time.

Robert L. Wrenn, Ph.D.
Professor Emeritus
University of Arizona

Preface

Instinctively, I would rise early in the morning and go into the dark, quiet living room to mourn. My seventeen-year-old son Roberto had just died of injuries received when he was hit at a crosswalk by a careless driver.

First, I would just sit in the dark crying and trying to keep my heart from disintegrating. Then I would take out my journal and write whatever would come from my wounded soul. The morning was a good time to write. Everyone else was still sleeping and I could allow myself to enter into the abyss of grief and express on paper what I could not express with the spoken word.

In the beginning I felt as if my pen was writing with blood instead of ink. Under the weight of such tremendous loss, I could not even imagine that I would ever be free of the excruciating pain that I was feeling. Eventually, I was to learn that, although grief never ends, it changes through the years and gradually becomes part of who we are as human beings; it changes from a deep pain to a sweet and gentle pain that serves to remind us of our loved one.

I have continued my morning writing during the more than three decades since the death of my son. Some of my words have become books, including one about our family's loss. I called it, *Goodbye, My Son, Hello*. It recounted the arduous journey through grief that we were taking. Through the years I have also written about my son's death in other books. When the *Goodbye* book was published it sold out and was not reprinted. I have had many requests for that book, especially from families that have suffered from the loss of a child. But rather than republish the original book, I have written this book: *A Grief Revisited: Weaving Loss into the Fabric of our Life*. This is not a sequel to the first book, but rather a look back over the decades of our family's life in light of the seminal loss we experienced when Roberto was killed. Although this new book includes excerpts from the *Goodbye* book and from other books I have written since, its emphasis is on how our family, mainly myself, have incorporated that early loss into the rest of our lives. It includes examples of how we transcended and transformed our tragic loss into purposeful living.

A Grief Revisited was written for anyone who has suffered the death of a loved one, but especially those who are in the first five years of bereavement. It is intended to give hope to those who believe, as I did, that they will never escape the black hole into which they have been cast by life. It is for those who see no light at the end of the long and lonely tunnel. And it is for those who have concluded in the aftermath of their loss that their life is over.

There is no question that following a major loss, life as we have known it *is* over. We will never be the same person as before our loss. Yet, life has not ended for us; it continues without our permission. We do, however, have a choice between remaining mired in our grief or learning and growing through our grief.

A Grief Revisited is a very personal book because grief is a very personal experience. I dare authentic self disclosure in this book because the bereaved person reading it will have no patience for facades or euphemisms. Although I am a retired counselor and psychotherapist who used grief therapy in my practice, this is not a clinical treatise on thanatology or a lesson on how to grieve properly. It is simply our story of loss, grief, recovery, and moving beyond mourning to purposeful living.

Because I have excerpted passages from the *Goodbye* book, which dealt mostly with my personal response to Roberto's death, most of this book consists of my own story. I have, however, included several writings by and about my wife Judy and each of our three surviving children. These include words they wrote when their loss was fresh and words they wrote in retrospect more recently. I realized that without their input this book would be incomplete.

The major losses we suffer in life seem like mountains that cannot be traversed. Their shadow is cast upon us and we are overwhelmed with grief. This mountain of loss seemed too high for us to scale, too wide to circumvent, and utterly impassable. The only way to the other side of this mountain was through the tunnel of mourning; and unless we entered into the darkness, we would never have seen the light again.

We had no choice but to enter into the belly of the whale and stay there long enough to be transformed by the pain; and then to resurface with new breath and new life.

First and foremost, our grief journey was a spiritual journey because major loss forces us to turn within for strength and courage. The first part, *Deep Darkness / Faint Light*, enters deeply into the passion of loss, and then introduces glimpses of light that illuminate the road to recovery and transformation. The second part, *Grieving Soul / Healing Spirit*, moves through the initial stages of loss, including the agonizing experience of facing the death of a child. Even from the beginning, the experience is couched in spiritual beliefs that ease the pain and offer hope. The third part, A *Family Grieves / A Family Remembers*, looks back on more than three decades to recount our family's reaction to the loss and its effect on our individual lives. The fourth part, *Anguished Grief / Fond Remembrance*, tells of the importance of remembering our loved one who died. It emphasizes the need to return to the past in order to deal with the present. Memories recalled (both good and bad);

promote healing through honoring and forgiving. The fifth part, *Meaningful Loss, Purposeful Life,* tells of our human capacity to give purpose and meaning to the inevitable suffering that comes with loss. It tells of how the worst thing that ever happened to us was converted into motivation for living fully and serving selflessly. The sixth part, *Endings and Beginnings,* focuses on our inherent ability to move beyond our grief and begin to invest in life again. It tells of the perpetual nature of grief, but also of its diminishing intensity as time passes.

My hope is that these words may be useful to those of you who are newly bereaved by offering hope that you will not only survive your profound grief, but will thrive on the other side of it. May this book serve as one of your helpful companions as you travel the path of solemn sorrow.

Child of My Soul

Child of my soul, I miss you so. Even now, I yearn for your presence. You were me and I was you. When you died, I also died.

Child of my soul, I come to you with a grieving heart. Mine is a shattered existence. I live in a world that is not real because you are no longer in it.

Child of my soul, you suffered so, and the end of your pain brings peace to my heart. How helpless I felt as your body succumbed to the shadow of death. Would that I could have taken your place. And yet, you are the one who is gone, and I am left with a broken heart.

Child of my soul, these have been times of desperation, pain, and agony. There have been days darker than hell itself. The reason to go on has left me, and I have questioned the point of it all.

Child of my soul, I was your parent, your protector, your security. But I could not protect you from this. I could not keep you safe from this. Please forgive my limitations, please forgive my powerlessness. Please forgive me.

Child of my soul, forgive my need to cling to what has been. I am just beginning to understand. Your life was gift. It came and touched the lives of others. It came and left love in its wake. It came and changed my life forever. Then it left, never to return.

Part One
Deep Darkness
Faint Light

Shadow of Death
Valley of Grief

Our seventeen-year-old son Roberto was barely hanging onto life with the help of a breathing machine. Even this artificial breath gave me hope that he would survive. For two days and two nights I hoped as I had never hoped before. Then the word came from the doctors: there was no more hope. Our family had to let him go. He died on Independence Day. The world turned dark for me that hour and that darkness would be my companion for some time to come.

The heavens cried with me that dreadful summer day. As the rain fell hard on his casket, the priest uttered familiar and comforting words: "Even though I walk through the valley of the shadow of death, I fear no evil, for you are with me; your rod and your staff, they comfort me" (Ps 23). Our firstborn was dead and now we had to bury him. Surely we were walking in the valley of the shadow of death. What could be more excruciating than the loss of one's child? A life of promise had been snuffed out like a candle in the wind. A promising future had been ruthlessly cancelled. Now only his past was left for us to have.

I dared to walk through the darkened valley of death and mourning because I believed that eventually I would come out on the other side, profoundly wounded and extremely vulnerable, yet still alive. I believed that God would guide me through the dreadful darkness. But my faith in God did not shelter me from feelings of anger, doubt, and devastation. Rather, it enabled me to gradually open to these very real and necessary emotions. Eventually, I would feel joy again, but not without first being weighed down with heavy sorrow. Eventually, I would experience the ecstasy of God's presence, but not before feeling the agony of abandonment. I would not flourish again until I had first been pruned back to my essential self.

My journey of grief would be a perilous trek, yet deep within I did not feel afraid. Even while walking in the shadow of death I knew that God was within me and without me. I felt defended against the internal wolves of fear and anxiety, and guided on the rugged path that was now my life.

The rain continued to pour on Roberto's desert grave. Now it was time to go – without him. It was time for us to say goodbye. With the activity of the funeral service over I had to face the reality before me. On the way home from the cemetery I meandered through the city under darkened skies. A million thoughts raced through my mind. Nothing seemed real. How could my son just stop being? My soul was gutted.

As I look back on those heart-wrenching days, I realize that at times I covered my grievous emotions by "being for others." I became the strong one to everyone in the family, offering solace and support. In order to be strong and available, however, I had to suppress much of what I was feeling. This, of course, led to a depressed state of mind for a while. One day I was snapping at my wife and kids for every little thing. I finally managed to alienate everybody. When they left to go shopping I stayed behind. I just stood there immobilized. Something was terribly wrong. What was happening to me? I went into the bedroom and began punching my bed and pillow with both fists, crying at the same time. I slugged with all my strength. A tremendous reservoir of anger erupted as if from a volcano. My tears were mixed with rhetorical "whys?" I continued beyond exhaustion until I collapsed on the bed. I felt exhilarated, washed out, unburdened. After that I was more aware of my emotions and expressed them tearfully to those whom I trusted.

My grief opened me wide open. Never before had I felt so vulnerable. It was at this shattered place in my life that I recognized the God of my soul. In my woundedness I was open to healing; in my brokenness I was open to wholeness. Perhaps it was my wounded spirit that was the last to heal. For so long during my grieving I had been unable to pray. But the nature of my prayer did not matter as much as that I prayed. Some days my prayer consisted of nothing more than a sigh of surrender or a silence of communion. God was in my suffering and in my healing.

Painful Absence
Compassionate Presence

In the midst of the most dreadful experience our family could ever have, we were carried by the demonstrated love of family, friends, neighbors, and members of our faith community. They heard about our son's accident and they came hurrying to the hospital to be with us – and for us. The waiting room was filled beyond capacity most of the time, even during night vigils. They came to offer us their compassionate presence.

My heart overflowed with gratitude toward these angels of the earth. I wrote them an open letter to express my appreciation.

Dear friends,

The death of our son brought about, if only for a little while, a gathering of angels.

They began to come even in the early hours of the tragedy. The priest who loves beyond measure came not only to console, but also to enter into the suffering himself. He would stay with us through the ordeal. The word spread like wildfire, calling forth those who would come to the hospital bringing with them their concern, their prayers, and their love for Roberto and his family.

The hours at the hospital dragged on and even the smallest, most insignificant sign became a seed of hope among those who waited so patiently and so faithfully.

The Angels came in the form of friends bearing gifts of food to nourish and strengthen us. They offered a shoulder to cry on; and they mixed their tears with ours. Late into the night these angels kept vigil. Some spent the night on short, bumpy couches; others left for a short time to check on their own families only to return to be with us.

Words were few among the angels. The grief we shared made us one in spirit; words seemed only to get in the way. One man shook his head in disbelief. A woman immersed herself in prayer. A couple sat near us in total silence and total presence. These unspoken words were salve to our wounded hearts.

There was the angel who prayed over our son as if he were his own. Another watched over our other children and our home while we were at the hospital. There was the angel who kept his head about him. He helped us to ask the questions that needed to be asked, and to make the decisions that needed to be made. Still another maintained a businesslike manner to help us with the necessary arrangements, while inside, his heart was breaking for us.

Other angels lent their singing voices. There were those who cried with us at the separation of death, but then rejoiced with us at the union of souls. Angels gathered for one last celebration of the life of Roberto and of his new life and they sustained us with a love that never dies. After the services angels prepared and served food for the visitors and offered to help in every possible way.

The pain will last a long time and the memory of Roberto will live forever because we love him so. But we will make it. I shudder, though, to imagine having gone through this dark night without the support and consolation of our community; without being able to share our burden with those who loved us in our time of greatest need.

I believe in God; I believe in Love; and I believe in Angels.

The Anguish of Loss
The Comfort of God

I had been taught that God was all-powerful, all-knowing, all-generous, and always present. Why then would God allow me to undergo the torture of loss? Of what good was it to me that God had all those attributes if I was to be left bleeding on the battlefield of life? Where was my sorrowful heart to turn for solace from the pain of separation and the agony of grief? To whom could I go to help me bear this horrendous burden?

Scripture says "Blessed are they who mourn, for they shall be comforted" (Mt 5:5). These words did not say to me that because I mourned the pain of my loss would be alleviated. On the contrary, they said clearly that if I mourned, that is, if I dared to allow myself to let go and experience all that came with grief, then and only then, would I find the comfort I desperately needed. The comfort that came to me when I entered fully into mourning was in the form of spiritual strength and sustaining courage. The comfort did not bring about restoration nor did it make everything all right again. Instead, it was a comfort that raised my eyes to look beyond that which could die to that which could not.

The comfort of God was not manifested in the granting of my wishes, but in my resolve that I would make the best of whatever came my way. The comfort of God was not manifested in a divine vigilance that protected me and my loved ones from all harm, but in the immanence of God that would follow me even into the hell of separation. I set aside my expectation that God would protect me and my loved ones from death. Instead, I realized that in my grief I was one with God who shared the agony of my loss.

The skies grow dark and bad times menace; and I am tempted to despair. Yet, through the clouds and the adversity comes the comfort of divine encouragement.

The comfort of God also came to me through the compassion of others. Often, it was not the consoling words but the secure hug of a friend or the gentle touch of a friendly hand that helped me. Occasionally, the well-intentioned said things that were not helpful at all. Clichés and statements advising me to accept "God's will" were especially bothersome to me. It was absolutely not consoling for me to hear that it was God's will that my son should die. Even with the purpose of alleviating my indescribable pain, I could not bring myself to blame Roberto's death on the will of God. Putting the tragedy at God's doorstep would certainly have placed it beyond injustice. Calling it "God's will" would have taken it out of the realm of human mistake or accident. But the reality for me was that bad things, horrible things, do happen to us sometimes and we are left horrified, devastated, and broken-hearted. Deep down I believed that God did not want my son to die anymore than I did. Instead of willing his death, God was mourning with me, hurting with me, crying with me, and keeping vigil with me through the night.

People offered from what they had, including their own brand of religion. Even as my son lay dying in a hospital bed, a devout woman saw the tears of desperation on my face and asked me, "Where is your faith?" I knew intellectually that she was sincere and meant to be supportive, but her question pierced my already wounded heart. Apparently, she believed that crying or displaying other strong emotional reactions to loss indicated a lack of faith. My truth is that strong emotional reactions and faith are not mutually exclusive. During my time of bereavement I adopted an attitude of gratitude and forgiveness toward those who meant to help me, regardless of what they offered.

For me, the comfort of God was not manifested in the power to bring the dead back to life, but in the power within me to sustain even the greatest of losses. The comfort of God was not manifested in the elimination of my excruciating pain, but in my faith to keep on living and loving even in the aftermath of death.

The comfort of God came to me through a heart filled with hope. My hope transcended what was before me, not by thinking about the future, but by daring to stay in the present and finding God's love in the eternal now. My hope was that, no matter what was to happen to me, there was a part of me that could not be violated, subdued, or killed – my soul.

Dark Night
New Dawn

Only when I acknowledged that my loss was real and irreversible did I begin to forge a new life. Although I could not separate my life from the circumstances which I faced, I knew in my heart that my life was not dependent on my circumstances, but on the nature of my soul. This necessitated deep prayer and mindful living. Through God-consciousness I was able to transcend my circumstances; and by living in the moment I was able to stay grounded and fully alive.

My darkest hour seemed an unlikely time for the birth of enlightenment, yet it was in the depths of the abyss that I encountered my essential self. Through the agony of grief I grew in self-awareness. Though blinded by tears of sorrow, I came to understand. Though humbled by the enormity of loss, I dared to move ahead. I could not shake the grief, nor did I want to, but gradually the night gave way to dawn and the day called me to life once more.

It is a paradox of life that when we are most broken, we have the greatest opportunity for wholeness; when we are lost in darkness, we can see even the faintest glimmer of light; and when we are deepest in the pit of despair, we discover there the roots of our faith.

Like the Phoenix rising from the ashes of loss, a new person came forth. My face and body had not changed, but inside I was different. I did not recognize the new person, but I liked him better. There were fewer pretenses, less vanity, less patience for the false and the wasteful. The new person seemed more humble, more approachable, and more simple.

I thought that I had lived and loved adequately before; I thought I had tended to relationships sufficiently before; I thought I had been compassionate toward others before; I thought I had engaged fully in life before. Well I was wrong. Only after my great loss did I realize that I had been living half awake.

I passed through the deep darkness of grief and came out on the other side more awake than ever before. I now faced my new life as a great adventure. I felt love more deeply, relationships became more precious to me, and I was more capable of compassion for those who were hurting.

From the ashes of lost dreams rose new ideas and intuitions. As I opened myself to what might come, I became aware of lessons learned and growth experienced through my loss. I felt an ocean of compassion flowing from my broken heart, and a powerful force impelling me to respond to the cries of wounded souls. It was beyond my willpower to avoid the suffering that had come my way, but it was my will and my intention that would direct my response to all that suffering.

I opened to all that the world had to offer. I accepted the caring support of others; I allowed myself to be carried spiritually beyond myself; and I experienced the raw emotions of a bereaved father. I opened myself up to the creative expression of my grief. I went back to school to be trained as a counselor and psychotherapist; I trained and worked as a grief therapist; I wrote books about grief and loss; I offered seminars for the bereaved; and I gave meaning to my loss by deciding that it would not be in vain. I allowed my loss to be a catalyst for healthy change.

Part Two
Grieving Soul
Healing Spirit

Facing Reality
Accepting Change

There was a dramatic difference between accepting the fact that my son was dead and accepting his death. Intellectually, I knew that Roberto had been involved in an accident and had not survived. Emotionally, I refused to allow the facts to destroy my life.

My son, my son, I love you so. Try as I may to understand why you have left me, my mind grasps not the meaning of it all. I did not know that this much pain could be felt by one man's heart.

I was left poor, weak, and in excruciating pain. I wanted desperately for it to end, but it could not end. There was no other way but through the dark tunnel of grief.

In the wake of loss, the fact that death was a part of life was little consolation for me. All I knew was that a bomb had fallen on my life. It had exploded my dreams into a million pieces, along with my relationship with my son, and my sense of order.

Everything seemed so unreal. What would life be like now? Would I survive this blow that had crushed my very being? What of the rest of my family? They were hurting terribly also. Every time I closed my eyes to rest a while I dreaded having to open them up again only to realize that it was not a nightmare from which I could awaken. It was real. My son, whom I loved so very much, was dead.

The car that struck and killed my son also killed a part of me. Where once there was innocence within me, and a carefree expectation of security, I now saw danger everywhere; and life meant vulnerability. When Roberto died my seamless existence was torn asunder. My illusion of permanency evaporated. I had known the beauty, harmony, and order of life. Now I also knew its ugly underbelly, and the dissonance and chaos that are part of life. In the midst of my despair I lost my trust for the future. I was tempted to leave the world, to withdraw from others and even withhold my love. Feeling empty of purpose and full of self-pity, I stayed stuck in my grief for quite a while.

When I lost my son I also lost the opportunity to be actively caring about his welfare, to be vigilant about his safety, to be enthusiastic about his achievements and joyful when I saw him happy and smiling. But I had not lost my sense of responsibility for him and for his future. This was frustrating because I did not know what to do with all that paternal energy.

The reality was that my dreams for Roberto had died with him. Never would I see him again. Never would I talk or walk with him, make plans with him, or hear him call my name again. Never would I see him be graduated from high school or college, and never would I witness his marriage or experience his manhood. Never would I hold his child on my lap. Never would he be with me again.

Even that which was lost to me from the beginning, which was never mine to lose, must be grieved. Dreams that were never realized and plans that were never executed must be grieved. I have had to let go of the dreams I had for my son. I have had to let go of life as I would have preferred it; yet, I have not let go of that indestructible Being within me from which comes solace, hope, and purpose to go on living.

Allowing Sorrow Emerging Transformed

As I responded to the death of my son I did not feel especially courageous, but in retrospect, it must have been courage that helped me to see it through. I had thought I knew my limitations, but circumstances proved me wrong. I was more capable of enduring my worst nightmare than I had believed. I overcame my presumed limitations, but only because I had to. I came to know the extent of my courage, but only because I was forced to confront and transcend my greatest fear.

Courage means the power to act from our heart. The courage that comes does not chase away fear and despair; it simply gives us the determination and perseverance to negotiate the dangerous corners and navigate the tumultuous waves.

I have heard it said that if we reach beyond our sorrow we will be transformed. I experienced this differently. For me, it was by staying in my sorrow, reaching into it and experiencing it fully that I was transformed. The transformation that happened to me was not an achievement for which I strived. It was the consequence of what I had experienced. I was changed by my loss whether I liked it or not. In the course of my transformation, I was compelled to let go of what could have been and to focus on what could still be.

I had been diminished by my loss, to be sure; yet, I had not been extinguished altogether. I could still choose to make the stone that crushed me the cornerstone of a new and better life. I was awakened to a life in which the fulfillment of desires did not satisfy my heart. No longer was it enough to be happy. My awakening through loss opened a window into a new reality. I saw things more clearly, I felt things more acutely, and I experienced life more robustly than I ever had before.

Roberto's death changed me in others ways as well. The loss experience taught me to simplify my life. I now dared to discard the superfluous and embrace what was near and dear to me. In simplicity, I measured my moments and used them well; while, at the same time, I opened myself up to the splendor of spontaneity. It was the ultimate irony that from the deep darkness of death I was thrust into the glorious light of life.

The death of my son had opened up everything to question and doubt. I had been so sure about so much before. Now I had lost my trust in old beliefs. Now I doubted my previous assumptions about order, about justice, and about rules. A safe world had turned dangerous. What had been dependable was now unpredictable. What had been stable was now fragile. No longer cold I take life for granted. Now it was a precious commodity that had to be cherished and appreciated one moment at a time.

For a long time my life seemed disordered and chaotic. Something had to give, and that was me. I was forced to change in order to survive. But the change had to come, not as a result of a geographical move or a jump to a new job; rather, it had to come as a result of facing off directly with what had happened in my life.

Roberto's death was a severe blow to my soul, and initially I took refuge in my isolation from the world. In my woundedness, I did not want to love again, lest I lose again. For a while I refused to get close to anyone, lest I be forced once more to say goodbye. I would have remained in this condition were it not for the nature of suffering. I had retreated to lick my wounds and to curse my damned misfortune, but as I felt the sorrow and endured the agony, the walls of isolation began to fall away. In my suffering I was one with all who suffer. I realized that the universality of suffering bound me to all humanity.

The focus on suffering which your death brought to me, my son, has surfaced the profound compassion I have always felt for those who live in the pain of poverty, illness, and loneliness.

Compassion is the power of my heart that prompts me to be nonjudgmental, merciful, kind, forgiving, patient, accepting, and understanding. It is the energy of love that moves through me and toward others. It is a force that compels me to act on behalf of those in need. Compassion invites me to enter into the poverty, hunger, illness, and grief of the world.

God suffers when any part of creation suffers. And because God is in my soul, the compassion I feel toward this wounded world is God's compassion moving in and through me.

Living Grief
Living Life

Suddenly I awoke in a new world, a world in which Roberto no longer existed.

What was lost cannot be restored. I understand and internalize this more each day. Where once my son was a part of the world I knew, I must now adapt to a world without him.

Some days I clung to my grief because I believed it was the last thread that connected me with Roberto. I believed that if that thread were to break, my connection to my son would also break. On other days the grief hurt so much that I would have done anything to take it away. I did not turn to alcohol or other drugs, instead, my drug of choice was writing. I threw myself into a book I had been working on before the accident. Ironically, the book was titled *Wholeness*, but now I found myself adding a new chapter about *brokenness*.

Tears are signs of life that rise from the wellspring of the soul. Tears are gifts from God that cleanse and salve our wounded heart. The profound sorrow that overcomes us in an hour of grief brings with it the tears of life that moisten even the driest of deserts. Tears emanate from the strength of spirit that dares to be vulnerable. Tears are not a sign of weakness; rather, they are a manifestation of the courage it takes to be fully human and fully alive.

I found that I needed a lot of time to myself to allow all the feelings of grief to surface. Whenever I got too busy or did not have some time alone my grief was dammed up and I became depressed. I welcomed the moments in which I could experience and express my grief. Of course it was not as if I could control the grief. It came whenever it wanted and picked its own way in which to manifest. When I least expected it, I would be overwhelmed by a storm of pain and sadness.

Initially, I didn't give a damn about using my grief experience as a catalyst to change into a better person. I was not interested in using this adversity to transform my life. At the same time, I knew that I could not remain the person I had been before the death of my son. That person no longer existed. And yet, even as I changed I had to be careful not to try to control who and what I might become. I could only observe and accept the person who would emerge.

Some days the psychic pain was more than I could bear. I remember looking forward to sleep because then the pain would be placed on hold, if only for a few hours. But bedtime also meant the end of another horrid day. Although it had never been an option to give up and succumb to the tragedy that had befallen us, sometimes I wished I could stop being so I would not hurt anymore.

I had hoped that in the mere passing of days and nights my painful grief would also pass, but I learned early on that time is neutral. By itself it accomplishes nothing. I discovered that it is not time that heals, but what we do with the time. My loss had to be fully mourned, and if it wasn't, time would just stand still. When I purposely tried to induce grief, no grief would come. Eventually, I learned to just stay open to grief and welcome it when it came.

At first I thought life would stop for me so that I could grieve – but it would not. As time passed, I realized that I had to mourn *and* live at the same time. I could not wait for the grief to end before I could begin to live again. I could not wait for conditions to be just right for the transformation to start. I could not put my life on hold while I mourned. The horror I was living was unwanted life but it was life.

As the months and years passed, my pain and sorrow changed, but it did not go away; it just became a part of my life. In the beginning it seemed that my grief was my total life. Eventually, it became just a part of my life.

To this day I feel the pain of grief for Roberto, but the pain is different. It is sweet and even friendly. It is no longer a pain I attempt to avoid through repression. It is a part of who I am today and who I will always be.

Surrendering Control
Finding Equanimity

Through my loss I learned that I had no control whatsoever over the events of my life. I did, however, have control over my response to those events.

As long as I held on to my expectations of how life should be for me and for my loved ones, I encountered frustration, anxiety and depression. In addition, I had learned the hard way that nothing was for sure. I could make plans and preparations, and this was wise to do, but life would do what it would do without checking with me first. In the years since the death of our son I have negotiated life differently than before. I still make plans, yet, I am no longer surprised when my best laid plans go awry and things happen very differently than I had planned. It is not that I have become cynical after my loss; rather, it is that I have lost my idealistic innocence and am more prepared for unexpected outcomes.

If resilience is the ability to thrive in the face of adversity, then I was not resilient at the beginning of my bereavement. I was lucky to just survive one day at a time. It wasn't until later that I felt the urge to move beyond survival and really thrive. It was not resilience. It was more in the nature of the death and resurrection cycles of life. The winter had brought death and loss. Spring had brought life and possibilities. Through the cycles I had changed in such a way that I was now open to whatever life decided to send my way.

The outcome of my life is more clear to me today than ever before. Still, I no longer take anything for granted. I can't rely on preparation, strength, or even a reservoir of faith. Rather, I must respond to the surprises of life from whatever the state of my soul is at the time.

For months after the death of my son I felt empty. It was as if the hand of death had reached into my chest and pulled out my heart. I was devoid of all that had sustained me in times past. I had entered the dark nothingness of faith. I felt myself dying to so much that I had been about before. Roles fell by the wayside, expectations dropped away, assumptions disappeared, and trust departed. I was dying to a world in which I had felt relatively safe and a life that had made sense. Slowly but surely, I let go of what would be and embraced what was, even if painful. Eventually, I began to let go of the security that the world had offered and turned instead to the only true security which I found within my soul.

I surrendered to life and to death. That is, I realized that my control over what would happen to me and to my loved ones was merely an illusion. My surrender was not the same as resignation; rather, it was a sober acknowledgement that life and death are forces of nature as wild and unpredictable as the wind. While they could not be controlled or manipulated, they had to become an integral part of my moment-to-moment awareness. To surrender myself to life and death meant that I not do battle with either. It meant that I find a way to live that would put me in harmony with the flow of life and at peace with the inevitability of death. In my surrender I became more accepting of life's events as they unfolded before me. The anger I had felt when things did not go my way subsided and, instead, I focused on what to do with my reality.

In my surrender I found equanimity. I began to respond less from my raw, emotional self and more from my centered, spiritual self. I realized that vicissitudes would be a constant in my life, and that the only variable would be my response. To be sure, I am still affected by what happens in my life, but instead of reacting to what is not, I respond to what is. I frame my days within a larger picture that includes more than my preferences and expectations of the way things should be. From a state of equanimity, I respond to life with more composure and less drama, no matter what comes. It is calm that emanates from the depths of my soul, a soul that has known great loss and pain and can therefore respond with a sense of balance.

Part Three
A Family Grieves
A Family Remembers

A Family Broken
A Family Restored

My wife Judy, our daughters Maria, 16; Cristina, 14; and our son Miguel, 11; and I had received much attention in the aftermath of the accident, but now everyone had left. The clatter of voices, the hugs and tears, and all the commotion gave way to an unwelcomed silence. It was a silence in which we had to face one another and try to make some sense of what had just befallen us. It was a silence in which we had to begin to redefine our family unit; and in which we had to confront the reality before us with no buffers, no veils.

Every human being grieves uniquely and this was true in our experience. Judy focused on researching the details of the accident in an effort to understand what exactly had caused such a major blow to our family. Maria became even more socially active than she had been before. Activity seemed to be where she found some solace. Cristina sought solitude in her room for some time. This helped her to grieve at her own pace. Miguel played a lot with his friends. Being at home was too sad for him. I coped by taking on the role of the strong one who took care of everyone else. This coping technique is not recommended because it interrupts the flow of grief and delays healing.

Sometimes I would imagine Roberto in his bedroom drawing political cartoons for the daily newspaper, a job he was so proud to have. When I imagined him there, I experienced a brief respite from that hollow sensation in my gut. Then reality would burst through my imagination and leave me devastated once again. His death just didn't make sense to me. He was a fledgling flower about to blossom that had been trampled back into the soil. He was a rare gift that was about to be presented to the world that had been snatched away by a thief in the night.

Our family made an early decision to not take any drugs during our bereavement. We were graced with the instinct to experience the hell of our loss totally and in the raw, lest we be derailed from the necessary grief through which we had to pass.

Fortunately, Judy talked a lot and I listened. She wanted to review details of the accident over and over. She wanted to understand what could not be understood; to explain the unexplainable. I was there for her, but I had no answers – only questions of my own.

We had heard that marriages usually don't withstand the loss of a child. Statistics seemed to be stacked against a couple making it through bereavement without the relationship being dramatically shaken or destroyed. I am not sure how we managed to beat those odds. Perhaps it was because we realized that early in our bereavement we were both too wounded to help each other with our grieving. Grief is so private and personal that, initially, except in the case of complicated grief which necessitates professional help, it needs to be done alone.

It helped that we dropped our unrealistic expectation that we could be strong for one another. Actually, there were times later on when we did help each other cope with feelings, but these were an unanticipated bonus. Another factor in the survival of our marriage through bereavement had to do with our ability to communicate with each other. This communication intensified during the first year of our bereavement and it did several things for our relationship. Not only were we able to express feelings without being judged, but we were able to keep up with each other's growth that resulted from the whole death experience.

The family talked about Roberto. We laughed at his antics, his idiosyncrasies, and humorous ways. Often mentioning his death to one another helped us face its reality. We talked about our individual relationships with Roberto. We discussed those things we were glad about and those we wished had never happened. As weeks and months passed, we consciously spoke of Roberto's characteristics and behaviors that we didn't like. We didn't want to idealize him, but to remember him as he really had been.

Accepting our family as a different entity was difficult. I became acutely aware of this when we received a free coupon for a family portrait. It had been eighteen months since our family had been suddenly thrust into change by Roberto's death. Yet, we were not prepared to acknowledge and confirm the change through a medium as brutally definitive as a photograph. A family portrait at this time would declare, "This is who we are now." We were not ready to face that reality.

Although something as concrete as a picture was too strong a statement for us to make at that time, we gradually began to acknowledge the reality of our new family group in more subtle ways. Slowly, but surely we began to reconstitute our family unit.

Judy
Roberto's Mother

Oh God. Where is my son? The early morning hours of July 1, 1982, were filled with confusion, fear, and eventually, shock as we learned of Roberto's accident. As we waited to find out his fate we were surrounded by family and friends who prayed and stayed at the hospital with us until we were told that he would not recover from his injuries.

Death, you level me to the core. You take away everything and leave me shocked and broken-hearted. What once was is now gone forever. Our sullen faces watch with brokenness and fear. Tears burst forth that cannot contain the pain of wailing emotions.

Roberto's celebration of life was filled with the spirit of God. It even rained the day he was buried, as if God were crying with us.

How can I complain when God is at hand to receive you Roberto, to embrace you? That is my only consolation, my only joy. Oh death, when you come, you leave life in chaos and desolation. Yet, I am called to celebrate the new life to which you carry my son. You are the chariot of fire that blazes through the living, taking those who have succumbed to a new dimension that is mystery, that is love.

Roberto had just finished his junior year of high school and had a talent for creating and drawing political cartoons. He had become editor of his high school newspaper and was scheduled to begin an internship with the local newspaper on the day he was buried.

In the beginning, my days were agonizing; tears, grief, and sorrow consumed me. I had so many questions that no answer would satisfy. I came to realize that I didn't have to understand in order to accept my new reality.

Roberto's death was my constant companion. Feeling fatalistic and extremely sorrowful robbed me of energy and of the ability to live fully.

I will not let you control my grief. I will not let you take over my life and rob me of living and loving. I will embrace the shadow of death and move into the sunlight of your eternal love for me. You have gone from my sight, Roberto, but not from my heart. Thank you for being my son.

Grief has a way of expressing itself and mine was to keep busy. Going to work and caring for my family at home helped ground me in day-to-day living. I had no enthusiasm for life. This was a time of profound sadness for me as I took my personal inventory as a mother and thought about the regrets that I had with my son. With regrets comes a sense of control. I was facing my future without Roberto.

Healing became my purpose in life. The way in which healing happens is always a surprise to me. I discovered that there was meaning in the suffering that I endured. It turned me inward to wrestle with my spirit and to feel the vibrations of life resonate within my heart and soul.

Death takes all that life has to offer and leaves behind the hope of everlasting love that transcends pain and suffering. The hope is in a greater love that only God has to offer.

I can attest to the truth that after the loss of a loved one life becomes ever more precious. Little things fade into the background and what is most important becomes a priority. Everything in my life was redefined: my relationships, my priorities, and my purpose in life.

Only God can direct his love through me and into the world once again. My children were growing, my husband became involved in his new career of psycho-spiritual counseling, and I used my experience as a mother who had lost a child to help others through a bereavement ministry. My heart became inspired to give, to reconnect with all that had been lost to me. The simple act of bringing forth the works of my hands and my imagination helped me to heal. I reached inside myself and responded spontaneously to that which wanted to be expressed.

I have grown in so many ways since your death, Roberto, and I'm sure that you have had a hand in it. By the grace of God I am making it through life. I am learning, loving, forgiving, tearing down what needs to be torn down and building up what needs my attention. My life is not perfect and I am learning to appreciate what is. I am open to feeling the vibrations of life resonate within my heart and soul.

Roberto made an imprint on all of us and we have carried his essence forward with us. I know he would be proud of us. I never thought I could say that I have been blessed by this tragedy in my life, but I know I have. I have been given the gift of compassion and a new way of looking at the world.

I know it has been a long time since Roberto's death. His brief life became the purpose for living my life fully. I know he is with me in spirit. I sense him in different ways. I wonder how he would be as an adult and what his life would be like today.

My life continues without the presence of my firstborn son. I am grateful for my husband, my children, and grandchildren.

With faith in God I strive to be conscious of life and of living and loving fully.

Maria
Roberto's Sister

Thinking back to the death of my brother, I think that
was the first experience of catastrophic loss for me;
any subsequent loss paled in comparison.

Before Roberto's death, I had played it safe as
the second born in the family. I got to stay in my
comfort zone without much responsibility. I
remember our family being solid. We did numerous
things together like vacations and family get-
togethers. As we got older we spent quality time
talking together as a family. I knew that we were
respected by our community and that we did
everything to help others who were less fortunate.
That's why I could never make sense of why bad stuff
could happen to such a family, our family, which
followed the rules and then some.

Being the one to discover that Roberto wasn't
home was the worst feeling ever. Had he not followed
the rules and stayed out too late? I guess that's what I
was hoping for, as opposed to something bad
happening to him. When reality finally sank in and we

had set up camp in the hospital waiting room, I still believed that all this was temporary. That's all my brain could wrap itself around at the time.

Waves of people would come in and out; people praying, crying, talking in whispers, trying to make sense of it all as well. At one point I remember crying in the bathroom, begging God to let me trade places with Roberto. I remember stupidly saying that I was going to go home and make him his favorite date nut cookies. Then the moment came when we were all summoned by the doctor into a tiny conference room. I just knew that he was going to say that Roberto was going to eventually come out of his coma and would need tons of rest – but that's not what happened.

I remember walking out of that room in disbelief, not knowing what to do. I think I ran into a family friend and just hugged her and cried. I remember thinking, "But I haven't made his cookies yet!"

Then came the funeral, my return to school, having to adjust to my new position as the eldest child, and being the first to graduate high school. It was a lot of pressure. I didn't draw for the school newspaper, I wasn't funny and quick-witted. I didn't want people feeling sorry for me. I began to care less about grades. I had an incentive to keep them up before because Roberto and I had a friendly competition, but now I was alone and I didn't care.

Eventually I got back on track with academics. Joining dance was helpful for me; it gave me a sense of purpose, something that I could be good at. Theatre followed and eventually I found a balance that worked for me. I wrote in my journal, including dreams I had of Roberto, dreams that helped bring me closure. I hung on to anniversaries for a long time so that I wouldn't forget what had happened. I even moved into Roberto's room and made it mine with dance posters and theatre records.

Through the years I have talked *about* my brother to whoever asks about my family, but I don't talk *to* my brother. I don't know why I don't. I don't like that it's harder to remember now and sometimes it seems like I never had an older brother. I keep a picture of him in my phone and my children know all about him.

Roberto's sudden death taught me not to assume that we will all live to be 95, that we all have a path in life, and not to take anyone for granted. I learned to say what I need to say now and not to assume that there will be a later time to say it. My last words to Roberto were, "Feed the dogs for me, okay? Thanks, bye." Not exactly what I would have chosen to say if I had known we would never speak again.

I believe my faith has gotten stronger, my chats with God more numerous. As I pray over my own children now I know that bad things can happen to beautiful people who follow the rules and are good.

Through the years I became more independent, stopped being so scared, and became more gregarious. I started doing things I wanted to do, like performing. I created a family that I love; and I now use my experience to help others when I can. As a teacher I use Roberto's experience creating comic books and political cartoons as an example for my students that they are capable of doing anything they put their minds to.

Sometimes I wonder how it would be to have the four of us siblings together today.

Cristina
Roberto's Sister

I was shocked to see my brother connected to so many tubes. He wouldn't wake up. He had severe brain damage. I don't remember praying, but I know we were expecting a miracle.

I remember sitting by my dad's side at the hospital; just the two of us on a lone bench. He wept. I had never seen my dad cry before. My pillar of strength had crumbled right before my very eyes. I was scared but stayed strong for him. My mom had many by her side. Everyone came to be with us.

My parents had to make the decision: if they allowed Roberto to live, he would be in a vegetative state; if they let him die, they would be able to donate his organs. Either way, our lives would be altered forever. They let him go.

I remember looking at Roberto's pale face at his wake. Why did he have to die? I wanted answers regarding the accident. They had it wrong. He shouldn't have died. It rained the day of his funeral. I still claim it was God's tears for us.

Our home was filled with guests and food for days. I hated the clichés that friends and family offered me. I knew they just didn't know what to say. When all that ended a huge void remained in our home. I hated that the world would keep going on. But life in the Quezada household also went on – one day at a time. I started high school. Roberto would have graduated high school that year.

We went to family counseling once. It wasn't for us. We were individually unique in our grieving. Roberto had given me his dog Bernie a couple of months before he died. Did he know intuitively that his death was coming? People tend to give their special belongings away before they die, right? Bernie ran away one night shortly after Roberto died. I remember praying fervently for God to bring Bernie back to me. He was all I had left of my brother. Two weeks later he came back. I was so thankful. When I was about 21, Bernie died and it was like my brother had died again.

Even though I am a very happy person, I think a part of me died with Roberto. I wonder what life would be like with him still alive. He was so smart and talented. I like to think that he's been watching over us all this time.

I have grown into who I am today in part because of my brother's death. It was a turning point for our family. A turn we didn't want to take, but a turn nevertheless. I would describe my life since he died as cautious. I am cautious with my life and with my relationships. I hold people whom I love very close. I tell my children that I love them all the time. I dread losing anyone else in my family, but I know it's a part of life. I strive to make good memories for my children individually and my family as a whole.

I try not to worry about petty things in life. I believe there are more important things to focus on. While I was raising my children, it was more important for me to spend time with them than to be away from them.

I often wonder what life would be like if Roberto was still around. Would he be married, have children, be working for Disney Studios like we all thought he would? Where would any of us be if that turn wasn't taken in our lives? This is what we were dealt. This is how we managed. This is our life.

Miguel
Roberto's Brother

Ever since I can remember, I have tried to find the silver lining to every circumstance. When Roberto was in the hospital dying I was very sad, of course, yet, at the same time I was learning how supportive friends can be. I learned that friends can be like family members. So many friends came forth to be for us during this crisis. They cared for us and nurtured us when we needed it the most.

With Roberto's death I learned that life is fragile, and that it is not guaranteed for a particular period of time. I remember being very sad. I recall the absence of Roberto from our life. Not only was he gone, but his talents that were beyond his years also went away. There was a void. There was so much promise that had gone away.

I was eleven years old when Roberto died. At that age everything was about me. I appreciated attention being paid to me. At the hospital and afterwards everyone was looking out for me. I got more attention than ever. It was so comforting to have friends and family taking care of me.

After Roberto died I remember that the family chemistry went away. It seemed as if each of us went to our own corner to grieve in our own way. I was focused on sports. That helped me cope. I became more responsible. I took on other responsibilities, like academics.

We were all so proud of Roberto and we are still proud of him today. There is still a sense of pride for us when we look at his drawings. From the beginning, I wanted to emulate Roberto, but I wanted to do it in a different way, according to who I was.

I felt that with his success so early in life there was an expectation for me to succeed as well. Perhaps it was competition or encouragement to also do well. I guess it was more of a family dynamic that I was going by; a belief that I had the resources and the tools to do whatever I wanted. I suppose I have passed on the same encouragement to my daughter Sommer.

Roberto continues to influence our lives even now. Recently Sommer, who is a high school freshman, learned that the same teacher who taught Roberto in high school was a substitute teacher for her Spanish class. When that teacher learned that Sommer was Roberto's niece, he praised Roberto as an excellent student. Even though Sommer had never met her uncle, she felt a sense of pride to be related to him.

Coincidentally, on that same day Sommer received an assignment from her English teacher to write a story about a super hero. Sommer decided to write her story about a hero from the Star Wars trilogy, but she knew little about Star Wars because it was popular before her time. Well it just so happened that I had saved a comic book that Roberto had written and illustrated about Star Wars for his high school English class, and for which he had received an "A." Sommer was able to use it as a resource for her assignment. After all these years, here was Roberto helping us in that moment. It helped Sommer to realize that she was not the first Quezada at that high school and it gave her a boost in confidence.

I felt a sense of abandonment when Roberto died. We had shared a bedroom. There was a sudden change, a sense of loss. I have used that sense of abandonment to remind me to be for Sommer and not abandon her in any way.

Roberto's life and death have influenced me through the years. I am very aware that bad things can happen to people, and that life can end in an instant. That has made me protective of Sommer, lest something harmful happen to her. Of course, I need to be careful not to overdo it.

As an adult, I realize that death can impact and change families in negative ways. I am appreciative that it didn't do that to our family.

Grief and Remembrance

My soul is gutted, my heart rent,
this day of grief and sad remembrance.

I have loved and I have lost,
speak not to me of consolation.

Like the grass of the field and the clouds
in the sky, ephemeral is the flesh.

I curse the darkness that overcomes me and
the blow that shatters the world I have known.

My days were filled with the joy of presence,
now I know only the sorrow of absence.

How deep the wound, yet
how resilient the spirit.

Through pining tears I see new light.
How slow my soul is to return.

My mind is filled with memories,
and my heart begins to mend.

While who I was has also died,
my loved one lives within me.

The world will never be the same,
a certain piece is missing.

Yet, I will dare to live again,
to love and risk the losing.

Part Four
Anguished Grief
Fond Remembrance

Evoking Memories
Building Bridges

In the first few weeks and months of my bereavement painful memories of Roberto's death flooded my mind. Memories reminded me that Roberto was gone. And yet, I did not want to lose the memories because, as painful as they were, they were all I had left of his life.

If we have been broken in days gone by, it is only by remembering what happened to us that we will begin to heal. Remembering means putting the pieces of ourselves back together again as we work toward wholeness.

Memories of Roberto came when I least expected, including the memory of his accident. I welcomed even the disturbing memories into my consciousness along with the emotions that followed in their wake. Sometimes recalling memories felt healing, often, it did not. In truth, the memories were all healing because they made me remember the reality of Roberto's life and death. It was not as if I could forget even if I wanted to. I was a bereaved father and mourning includes remembering.

Some say that such remembering is not healthy, that we ought not to dwell on thoughts that make us sad. Yet the opposite is true. Grief revisited is grief acknowledged, and grief confronted is grief resolved.

From the beginning, our family began to recall memories about Roberto. The memories were all we had left and we needed to share them with each other. It was painful to remember, and yet, the memories somehow eased the tension between us and mitigated the pain within us. We remembered his idiosyncrasies, his habits, his dry wit, and his moodiness. Roberto kept us entertained with his impressions of movie actors and his very realistic movie sound effects. We remembered his tendency toward perfectionism and his reluctance to do his chores. We remembered his passion for drawing and his dreams for what might come.

Evoking memories, though sometimes disturbing, connected us to the past. Our memories were the bridges we built from how it used to be to how it is today. They helped us to accept that our world had changed; and that, while we could visit the past, we could no longer live there. Memories were the treasures that we could hold in our mind for a little while and laugh, cry, or just ponder in silent reminiscence. Memories can help to heal our wounded heart, especially if we allow ourselves to experience and express the emotions they evoke.

Grief touches our lives in various ways. Sometimes it enters through the door of our memory: a certain song, a certain fragrance, a certain picture, will remind us of how it used to be. Sometimes it brings a smile, sometimes a tear.

I remember Roberto realistically. He was just beginning to blossom into a more mature person when he died. Sometimes he was downright mean to his siblings, but they still loved and admired him. He was also admired by his classmates. He had been named editor of the school newspaper for his forthcoming senior year, a year he would never experience. Although a quiet boy, he was witty and talented. Roberto spent hours alone in his room dreaming up and drawing the caricatures he would feature in his political cartoons.

Roberto was an integral part of our family. We needed him and he needed us. When he died the family was no longer whole. In a few short years

Roberto impacted the life of his family and the community in which he lived. He was an individual, but he was also a part of us and when he died, the family unit also died and had to be reconstituted.

I remember the night Roberto was born. It was 1:59 in the morning of New Year's Day. He was the third baby born in the city that year, but he was the first for us. I remember praying for guidance because I did not know how to be a father. I prayed that Roberto be healthy and happy with us. For seventeen and a half years he was our joy and sometimes our frustration. We were blessed with his presence in our life.

I miss your style, your smile, your frown. I miss the overflowing excitement you experienced with each of your accomplishments, but which you tried so hard to hide.

Lost Relationship
Deeper Bond

Perhaps the most difficult part of my bereavement was severing the emotional connection I had felt with Roberto. I not only had to grieve the loss of my son, but also the loss of the relationship that I had so enjoyed with him. But as I experienced the transformation of our relationship, I realized that the ties between us had not been severed, but made stronger. The relationship had merely changed from the seen to the unseen, and from communication to communion. It was not so easy to let go, yet I was being invited to transcend the loss of our worldly relationship by experiencing a different kind of love.

You would have me believe in the Whole from this, my brokenness; and you would have my love beyond the confines of the flesh. Grief can teach us that the loss of a loved one does not mean the loss of love; for love is stronger than separations and longer than the permanence of death. Going on with life does not mean that we must leave our loved one behind like some historic ruin. Our task is to include the past with the present and to let these two cornerstones be the foundation on which we build our future. While Roberto's life had already been an integral part of my life, it is his death and his absence that I am now integrating into my life.

I began to detach from Roberto, but only in the sense that I no longer clung to what had been while he was still alive, that is, his physical presence and my actual experience of him. Now I began to attach to him in a different way. Now I prepared a place for him in my mind and in my heart. His life as I had known it had changed, but my love for him continued unabated. I believed then, as I believe now, that death did not end our relationship, rather, it transformed it. Roberto lived within me and our relationship would continue to grow and deepen.

When we release what has been ours, it takes on a different nature. We may no longer hold it in our hands, but we can hold it in our hearts. We may no longer live it, but we can forever be mindful of it.

After Roberto died I was acutely aware of just how precious my time with him had been. I looked back and lamented that I had not allowed myself even more time with him. The things that kept me away from him seemed important at the time. Now those same things seem so unimportant. I learned not to take my close relationships for granted.

I have memorialized Roberto in my daily living. My work alleviating the emotional suffering of others has been done in his memory. I remember his finest traits and emulate them. I remember his finest aspirations and try to fulfill them in my own life and in my own way. Sometimes I remember him by going to his gravesite, although I have never really sensed him there. As I walk in the world in which Roberto no longer walks, I find creative ways to commemorate his life and his death. There is a place where I look at a mountain that prompts prayer and remembrance. I often pass the location of Roberto's accident. It is a terrible place; it is a sacred place.

You have gone beyond the reach of my senses only to return at the core of my being. Goodbye, my son, hello.

Regretting Mistakes
Forgiving the Past

Before I could completely release the past and form a new relationship with Roberto, I had to forgive him for anything I was holding against him, and to ask his forgiveness for the ways in which I might have hurt him over the years. I remembered not only what had been good between us, but also what had not. My relationship with Roberto had been a typical one between a father and son with high and low points. Since he was our firstborn, Roberto received the brunt of my overcautious, strict, and nervous parenting.

I did not always like you and the way you acted. I also know that you were not too crazy about me at times and with some of the ways that I treated you. There were probably some times when I was not supportive of you and who you were. For all the ways in which I hurt you, I am truly sorry. Yet even as I say this I feel a sense of peace about our relationship. I am thinking that in spite of times when were we were at odds with each other, there was always love. I believe that neither you nor life holds me to my debts.

As I released Roberto into death, I also released him from anything I might have held against him. I was fortunate that in the last twelve months of his life our relationship had been good. We had some shared interests and worked on them together. But there was still more forgiving to do. I found that I was still holding against myself the failure to protect my son against all harm.

I have felt so powerless because I was unable to prevent my son's death. Wasn't there something I could have done or not have done to change the course of events? Wasn't it, after all, my job as his father to protect him from danger, to keep him safe?

Perhaps this was the guilt that any parent feels when losing a child under any circumstances. It didn't matter that the charge I made against myself was unrealistic, I still felt guilty. It was a guilt that could not be dismissed through rational thinking or common sense. It was a guilt that could only be lifted away through self-forgiveness. I made the decision to forgive myself. I decided to no longer hold against myself my limitations as a man, as a father, and as a protector.

As I remembered my life with Roberto I did not exclude those parts of his life that were painful to remember. I remembered the love that we shared and the ways in which he brought me joy. I remembered his pleasantness and the pleasure of his presence. I remembered what I appreciated, but also what I regretted. There were some memories that haunted me until I was able to recall them fully, to feel the raw emotions that they triggered, and to forgive myself for my part in them. I had learned that wounds held by memories can heal through contrition and forgiveness.

Even though I believed that I had been forgiven by Roberto, my spiritual solvency would not be restored until I also forgave myself. Yet, forgiving myself was one of the hardest tasks I faced.

Self-forgiveness was not just a matter of saying "I forgive myself." It required sinking into the innermost room of my being and standing there naked before the universe. It required recognizing the error of my ways and expressing my sorrow. There, at the base of my existence, I came face to face with the God of my soul who refused my indebtedness. As I came to accept God's forgiveness, I learned to forgive myself.

Self-forgiveness was a decision to not hold against myself the errors I had committed, but it did not cancel out my responsibility. I still held myself accountable. I still faced the consequences of what I had done or failed to do, and I still worked hard to change myself in such a way that I was less apt to repeat my mistakes.

Releasing What Was
Embracing What Is

Roberto was just becoming a man. His life ended even as it began. He had been granted so little time to impact the world, but impact it he did. Even in his short lifespan he left his mark in my heart and in the heart of many others. The biography of Roberto was rich in creativity, imagination, hope, and dreams. I am aware of how blessed I was as his father to have witnessed his short, precious life.

I pray in gratitude that it was I who was selected to father Roberto. That fatherhood has undergone transition. No longer his mortal father, I am the father of an immortal being who is now and ever shall be.

There is more to remembrance than recalling the past. When I remember Roberto I am mindful of his effect on my life. I bring his life and his death into the present. I become aware of his physical absence and his spiritual presence.

I lost my son on one level and gained him on another. Now we share a relationship which knows no bounds of time or space or physicality. I feel closer to Roberto than ever before. He is now within me. I have internalized him. We are no longer in a concrete presence to each other. Now I feel a strong connection that transcends our life and death.

Roberto, my son, the memories of days gone by will fade for me as I go about the business of now, but the memory of your presence will never leave me. Quite simply, I will no longer dwell on your death. I will remember your life and what a great part of my life you will always be.

In my counseling and psychotherapy practice I would ask bereaved clients: "What part of you has died with your loved one, and what part of your loved one still lives on in you?" Pondering the answers to these questions prompted my clients to consider how they had changed and how they had incorporated the life and death of their loved one into their own life. I asked the same question of myself during my bereavement.

The part of me that died was my attachment to life; I died to my insistence on how I wanted things to be. I died to what had been so important to me: achievement, image, and control. It no longer mattered that I achieve, it only mattered that I live fully. It no longer mattered that I look good in the eyes of others; it only mattered that I be true to myself. It no longer mattered whether I had control of life, it only mattered that I control how I would respond to life. The parts of Roberto that lived on in me included his focused creativity, his fertile imagination, and his spirited perseverance.

You are the one who was killed, yet in my heart I feel I also died a little. You, Roberto, were a part of my flesh. Since I am also that of which you were, you continue to live through me.

It was by internalizing Roberto that I could truly heal my wounded heart. My healing came, not by forgetting my loss, but by integrating it into the fabric of my life. My healing came, not by separating myself from Roberto, but by internalizing him and letting him become a part of who I was. I could not live my son's life for him, but I could honor it through my own life.

The paradox is that by letting go of what we love, it is ours to have forever more. It seems that the integration of total life comes only when we have allowed the disintegration of its parts. It is because we say goodbye to what we love that it becomes a part of who we are.

Honoring the Memory

Even as we live our moments fully, we pause on
occasion to touch the empty place within our heart.

Those with whom we've shared our world
we know now but in spirit.

Our days continue, though theirs have ended,
yet, we do not forget.

Our life was changed by death,
yet death is part of life.

Grief will visit when we least expect,
as will the pain of remembering what is no more.

Joy will visit when we least expect,
as will the pleasure of remembering what used to be.

How precious the memories of our beloved;
how blessed to have partaken of their life.

Days pass and years accumulate, and we pause
on occasion to touch the empty place within our heart.

Part Five
Meaningful Loss
Purposeful Life

Finding Purpose
Giving Meaning

Being touched by death in this most intimate way forced me to stop and carefully examine what I truly wanted from life. Roberto's death shook the very foundation of my life and sent me searching for a purpose for which to exist and a meaning by which to live. But it was important that I not attribute purpose and meaning to my loss prematurely, lest I block the natural flow of grief. I was suspicious of any impulse, inspired or otherwise conceived, that might distract me from my grief. I was not to circumvent necessary mourning in order to give it purpose and meaning, rather, I had to experience the full impact of my loss before purpose and meaning could be found.

Finding purpose and meaning to my son's death came only when my distress had lessened and I had become better adjusted to the loss and to the new world in which I found myself. It was important that I understand why Roberto's death had happened in order to find purpose and meaning in it, but it was also important that I understand the impact his death had on me.

Before I could ask the "why," I needed to deal with the reality of loss and to get involved fully with the suffering that was to come.

The unexpected death of my son taught me the cruel lesson that the future is an unknown commodity. But one thing I knew for sure was that the rest of my life, however long, would not be wasted.

Finding purpose and meaning requires intentional living. It does not happen on its own. I could not look to others to tell me what purpose to assign to my loss or what meaning to attribute to it. It was up to me to transform my grief into a constructive purpose for myself and others. It was not a universal meaning that I sought, rather, it was a personal meaning, unique to whom I was at the time and to the circumstances that I faced.

There is a force within each one of us that emanates from the essence of who we are. This energy, this motivation is powered by a personal and unique purpose for living; a potent intentionality that gives meaning to our existence and fulfillment to our being.

My purpose and meaning could not be imposed from without. It was born of my nature, my personality, my experiences in life, my circumstances, my talents, interests, emotions, thoughts and, most of all, my beliefs. This was not an easy task. I had to search, find, and develop purpose and meaning in the light of my loss. It was my response to what happened. Finding purpose and meaning in the death of Roberto was possible for me only because the loss had already happened and could not be reversed. Suffering for the sake of suffering was no virtue; it was only because the suffering was inevitable that I could give it purpose and meaning.

We are like flowers in the garden of life, rooted in the soil of our humanity, growing toward the fulfillment of our purpose, and blossoming into what we were meant to be.

While I did not seek purpose and meaning in my loss in order to heal, finding purpose and meaning in it did indeed promote healing. By making my grief purposeful and meaningful I was able to avert despair and actually grow personally and professionally. My grief taught me that after being pruned by this loss, I could flourish again in season and bring forth the good fruit that comes, not in spite of loss, but because of it.

I found purpose in my loss by receiving from the world all that it had to offer. I accepted the caring support of others; I allowed myself to be carried by a spiritual force beyond myself; and I experienced the raw emotions of a bereaved father.

Attributing purpose and meaning to Roberto's death prompted me to do it to my whole life. I found purpose and meaning in the spectacular and extraordinary things around me, and also in the ordinary and mundane. Purpose and meaning were not limited to grandiose schemes and great accomplishments, it was also purposeful and meaningful to spend time with my family, and to be quiet and still so that my soul could commune with God. I found purpose and meaning in the special events of my life as well as the uneventful. Just "being" became purposeful and meaningful to me.

Being Pruned
Blooming Forth

The only thing that made sense to me about Roberto's death was that it made no sense at all.

Is there any order to this craziness? If my son could cease to live so abruptly, without logic or purpose to his death, what then was my life all about? What sense did it make that I was going on living?

Although it was clear that I could not free myself of the circumstances before me, I was free to respond to those circumstances in whatever way I chose. At first, I chose to respond as a human father – devastated by the tearing away of my very flesh. Eventually, I chose to respond as a human being who could accept impermanence as the basis of life, and love as a reason to go on living.

You, a part of my life, have been torn from me with the swiftness of a heartbeat and the agony of the cross. In my despair I ask, why go on? Why care about anything else? Why need I do the things of life if death deems them in vain? But no, my son, I will not despair, for your death will be my life. You would have me blossom where you have been pruned. You would have me enjoy the presence of a brother, smell a rose, and wonder at a hummingbird. You would have me do the things that I must do and use my moments well. You would have me remember the joy of having you, and yes, the pain of letting you go.

What a dreadful waste is the death of a young man on the cusp of a bright and fruitful life. If ever there was proof of randomness and chaos in the universe, this was it. Yet, it was in my power to take the randomness and give it a pattern, and to take the chaos and give it order. It was in my power to take that which made no sense and give it meaning, and to take that which was pointless and give it purpose.

Sometimes well-intentioned supporters told me that there was a purpose for my loss. This drove me crazy because I did not believe that. Even when I considered all the good that came of our profound loss, I would have gladly given it all up to have my son live. I could not be convinced that my son's death was a quid pro quo for some benefit to come to me or the world. I would not be a party to such a transaction.

What I did believe then, and believe today, was that once bad things happen to us, we have a choice either to be crushed into the ground or to eventually give meaning to what has happened and assign purpose to it.

My life had changed radically and I would no longer settle for anything less than a meaningful existence and a purposeful life. Life had let me down, and for some time I hated life and wanted to strike out against it. But as I lived through the deep darkness of grief my perspective of life had also begun to change. No longer was I expecting something from life, rather, life was expecting something from me. Life was not here to serve me; rather, I was here to serve life. No longer was I questioning the ways of life, instead, I was accepting life as it unfolded before me, and I was making the best of it.

It took some time to differentiate between the good that I could create from the consequences of my son's death and the causes of his death. I have come to understand that while my son's death was not caused so that any good would come of it, good indeed could come of it. Good is not born of evil; good rises from the ashes of evil. No reason, however good, was worth the loss of my son. But now that it is done, I can grow a flower in this desolate desert of my experience.

To grow a flower in the desert meant that I had an important role to play. I had rejected the idea that Roberto's death was part of a plan and that I had to simply accept it without question or protest. Instead, I believed that life was strewn with prosperity and adversity, life and death; and as I embraced life, I embraced all that came with it. Now it was up to me to enter into that desolate desert where life seemed all but absent, and till the arid soil with my trembling hands and water it with my pain-filled tears until the flower of hope began to grow.

Desert Flower

Desert flower so majestic,
blossoming among the thorns.

I am so much in awe of you.
You dare to grow where others dread.

In barren soil you germinate,
from the wasteland you burst forth.

What faith and hope are in your heart;
what courage and what patience!

Against all odds you struggle on,
you thrive in adverse weather.

You rise above the dead and dry.
You are the hope of all the world.

Being Vulnerable
Opening to Life

The death of my son was a powerful catalyst for the internal changes that would happen to me over the years. The loss led me to commit myself to a life of healing emotionally wounded souls. But before I could heal anyone else, I first needed to heal myself.

Much was taken from me, but in the process I learned to receive. I have always been a giver, but through this ordeal I also became a receiver. In quiet and repose I was open to the silence that healed and the rest that restored. I learned that it takes courage to acknowledge needs and even more courage to ask for them to be met. In the aftermath of loss I received the strength and courage to keep on living and loving.

I awakened to the present. If the death of my son had not awakened me, nothing else could have. I dared to remain in the now, to stay awake, and to watch and pray. To remain in the present allowed my soul to occupy my body. Staying in the present made me aware of my immediate surroundings and kept me living consciously. After all, the present moment was my only reality.

From this awakened state I could not help but treat others with loving kindness, concern, and justice. My awakened life prepared me to love constantly and to reach out compassionately to those who suffer and are in need. I became fully present to those in my midst.

My awakened life was willing to be simple, small, and slow. Life was too pure for me to complicate it, too real to exaggerate it, and too precious to accelerate it. My awakened life was grounded in profound peace and graciously carried with it the joy and the suffering that are part of living.

Elusive, unpredictable life; fulfilling, joyous life; you are pain and you are ecstasy. You span the eons that have been and are yet to be; it is in the present moment that you manifest through us.

I became vulnerable to all that came in life. I was more vulnerable than a newborn baby. I knew that if I could be hurt this deeply, and if my life could be affected this vastly, then I could survive any harm that came to me. The paradox was that through my vulnerability I became invulnerable. I could not be hurt more than this. I had been through hell and I could not imagine anything worse than what had already happened to me.

In my vulnerability I laid down the arms with which I had defended myself in the past: control, manipulation, and escape. Now I stood defenseless, naked, and alone before the fortuities of life. My faith did not assure me that all would be well, but rather, that no matter what happened, I would handle it. What could be harder than what I had already handled?

What is this state we call our life? Is it merely a dream? Will we come to know its secret? It is so fragile, and yet so vital; ethereal, and yet rooted in the depths of our soul. Life, we hardly know you, yet you hold us in the palm of your hand.

To cherish life does not mean that we cling to it. To hold it above all else does not mean that we are not prepared to lay it down. It is when we let go of life that we are free to live it. To lose our life for the sake of love is to save it for eternity.

Part Six
Endings
Beginnings

Dropping Expectations
Choosing Hope

There was a big difference between hoping and clinging to expectations. Expectations would impose my will onto life, while hope opened me up to accept life as it came.

When I chose hope, I let go of those expectations that would have set me up for disappointment and disillusionment; instead, my hope was placed in what had already been given to me: the courage to stay present and to engage my total self in the task of living. Hope was not a fixation that I had on the future even as I ignored and neglected the present; rather, it was in the present moment that I hoped. It was in the now that I committed myself to live according to my potential. It was time to open my soul to the ways of love. It was the moment to respond to life with vigor and purpose.

Through hope I acknowledged inevitable endings and welcomed the onset of new beginnings. Through hope I allowed the pruning of the old ways that inhibited growth, and I invited a more fruitful harvest in my life. The pain and suffering that were now a part of my life did not disappear by hoping; but hoping gave me the motivation and the wherewithal to transform myself. Hope was the spiritual energy with which I strove to overcome difficulty, resolve problems, and survive my journey through the valley of darkness. Hope was not a flight from despair, but a confrontation with it; and a confidence in my ability to transcend it.

My hope moves me from shallow life to the core of my humanity where I discover the dynamic forces of God's love.

Hope is that spiritual power that comes from deep within our soul. It becomes the energy that moves us through the day, daring to love in the face of a loveless world. With hope at our core we can live through whatever comes our way, and whatever loss life hands us. In the light of hope we can transform the greatest tragedy into fruitful life.

Along the pathway of grief I died to myself. It was not the physical death through which we must all pass, but the death that comes from surrendering to the transformative forces of life. By dying to who I had been, I released my hold on the fabricated self to which I had clung and plunged into the earthiness of life. As I moved through the deep darkness into new life, I encountered this paradox: to really live, I must first die.

Even in the face of suffering and death, I dared to hope because even there I discovered the potential of new life. I believed that, regardless of the conditions or circumstances of my life, if I hung on to hope I would overcome. My hope was that no matter what occurred in my life, no matter what happened to me, there was a part of me that, though capable of being wounded, could not be annihilated. My hope was in that pure and holy part, that invulnerable, indestructible vestige of life – my soul. It was my soul that emitted the life-force I call spirit. It was my soul that was willing to be terribly wounded in the name of love.

My hope, even in my darkest moments, is to become the expression of God in the world.

Broken Heart Awakened Heart

In the midst of my grief it was very hard to pray. Sometimes my prayer consisted of nothing more than a deep sigh of letting go or the silence of my surrender.

My spirit felt dry and I thought my faith was lost forever. Stripped to my bare essence, I experienced life nakedly. In this state of vulnerability I laid down my defenses, set aside my masks, and dropped away my fantasies. Only the reality of what was penetrated my mind. There was no reason to be more or less than I was – broken and devastated.

I haven't prayed, really prayed, recently. I am so conscious of the difference it makes in my life. I haven't wanted to pray from my heart. It makes me more vulnerable than I want to be. Prayer opens up feelings and emotions that I am trying to avoid. It brings sensitivity that I cannot afford. Of course this is nonsense. The truth is that I cannot hold back life itself anymore than I can hold back the rain. So I pause this morning to pray.

Grief opened me wide open, leaving me exposed to life. It was at this shattered place in my being that I encountered the confluence of spirit and soul, heaven and earth, life and death. It was here in the deep darkness that I began to see the light. Having lost the physical presence of my son, I was cast into this mysterious spiritual world where I could perceive through my more subtle senses. I became aware of that which transcends the outer world. I took refuge in my innermost consciousness, my most essential self, that secret place that is my heart. It was a broken heart, yet it had awakened to life as never before.

My awakened heart led me to begin reading a variety of holy writings. I became acquainted with the sacred traditions that have spanned the ages. I found there the empathy, understanding, comfort, and compassion for which I had been searching. I became more and more aware of my total dependence on the God of my soul for every aspect of my life. I prayed without ceasing, remembering God at all times. I rested in God at nightfall and rose before the sun to dedicate my day to God.

No longer is the spiritual a distant mirage; I feel it has engulfed my surroundings and penetrated all that is my life.

I surrendered to the force of God that unified my fragmented self. Here, I was united with my son who had lived and died, and also with all beings that have ever lived or will ever live. The paradox of my spiritual journey through grief was that when I embraced the reality of impermanence, I found the permanence of God.

Before the death of my son, my life was driven and future-oriented. I experienced joy occasionally, but not frequently and not unbridled. For some reason I was afraid to experience joy wholeheartedly. After the death of my son I knew one thing for sure: I would never again feel joy. But I was wrong. Even in the darkest days of mourning, glimmers of joy began to appear. When they did, I initially felt guilty because I was supposed to be grieving death, not enjoying life. But even before my tears of loss stopped falling and the heart pain subsided, joy made its return.

The joy that comes in the morning comes not in spite of the night, but because of it. This is the paradox of joy. It is not to be found separate and apart from the pain of life, but integrated with it as we live out our humanity. Joy is the rose that blooms among the thorns.

Awakened Heart

Mine is a poor heart. A heart once filled with the joy of my beloved's presence now is empty and desolate.

Mine is a broken heart. The wound of loss has left me shattered. The life we shared is now divided.

Mine is a humble heart. I assume nothing now. Death has leveled my highest aspirations. I have come to know my basic self.

Mine is a yearning heart. I pine and wail for my beloved. The absence overwhelms me. I hunger for his touch and thirst for just one glimpse of his embodiment.

Mine is a forgiving heart. I have left behind what did not matter. I have cancelled what was owed. Now I hold to just the memories, the rest I have released.

Mine is a single heart. Only one thing matters, all else is set aside. I dare not look away and lose the faith to which I cling.

Mine is a peaceful heart. It is a strange peace that I experience, a peace that comes when I have nothing left to lose.

Mine is a brave heart. I have sustained the greatest blow and have survived. Nothing else can hurt me now.

Mine is an awakened heart. No longer do I look toward my tomorrows or lament my yesterdays. The moment before me is what matters. Today is where I live.

Grief Never Ends
Grief is Absorbed

I needed to allow grief to come and to go naturally, but sometimes I clung to grief too long because I believed it was the last vestige of the relationship I shared with my son. In my bereavement I was not afraid of the future, but sometimes I was afraid that if I began investing in life and looking toward the future, I might end my involvement with my dead son who was no longer a tangible part of my life.

As days pass and memories grow dim, I struggle between looking to the future and holding desperately on to the past.

Although I knew that grief was a part of love, I also knew that grieving forever was not a sign of deeper love. The loss of my son interrupted my life, to be sure, but it was clear to me that a permanent interruption would not be indicative of permanent love. On the contrary, my love for Roberto was best manifested in the way I went on living my life.

When the intensity of my grief began to abate, I wondered sometimes whether I had mourned enough. Whenever I experienced even a glimpse of joy, I sometimes accused myself of forgetting my son. Of course this was not true. In fact, I discovered in my grief experience that glimpses of joy are moments of grace that come to give us respite from the intensity of grief. I was not abandoning my son; rather, the time had come for me to pass beyond my grief.

Through my grief experience I learned that when I could ponder the life and death of my son without inordinate emotional reaction, and when I could remember him without the psychic pain that I experienced in the beginning, I was well on my way to healing my wounded heart.

But I also learned that it was the nature of grief that no matter how much time had passed for me, and no matter how much life I had experienced, my heart would never be the same. If my grief was resolved, why did I still feel a faint sense of loss on the occasion of anniversaries and holidays? Why did grief still come when I least expected it. Why did I sometimes feel a lump in my throat even years after my loss? It was because moving beyond grief did not mean that I left my son behind. Healing my wounded heart did not mean that I had forgotten Roberto.

It is as if the ones we have loved and lost are determined not to be forgotten.

Some said to me that such remembering was not healthy for me; and that I ought not to dwell on thoughts that make me sad. Yet, for me, the opposite was true. I believed that grief revisited was grief acknowledged, and grief confronted was grief resolved.

The intensity of grief diminished for me over time, in part, because I allowed it to visit me from time to time. But I was aware that if the intensity of my grief had gone on longer than two years or if my life had been dysfunctional months after my loss, it would have necessitated professional help to get unstuck.

Grief taught me over the years that if I tried to deny the reality of a major loss in my life, I would end up denying other parts of my life as well. Grief also taught me that the loss of my son did not mean the loss of my union with him.

Grief, which I have come to know as the other side of love, has not disappeared for me completely. It has become a part of who I am. It isn't that my old friend grief wants to get in the way of my living; it just wants to stop by and visit for a while. It comes to remind me that I can survive even the greatest of losses. Most of all, my old friend grief reminds me of the impermanent nature of life, of the importance of appreciating every moment of every day, and of cherishing my loved ones above all.

My old friend grief may leave me for a while, but it will return to remind me that love is stronger than separation and lasts longer than the permanence of death.

Child of My Soul

Child of my soul, your death is a reality. Yet, even from this unacceptable reality can come new life. What is the lesson I can learn? What purpose can I give this horrific loss? What meaning must I find? I will not let you die in vain. I will draw from your life, and I will draw from your death as I continue the journey before me.

Child of my soul, so much has been taken from me. I feel poor and desolate. Yet so much is left behind. My heart remembers you. There are memories of joy and laughter; there are memories of pain and tears. There are memories of times together; and there are memories of times apart. The memories of my days with you will sustain me through the night.

Child of my soul, I release you unto eternity. I let go of anything that binds you to this world. You are love, you are spirit, and you are free. No longer will I know you as before. Gone is your touch, your face, your presence. Gone are the plans, the dreams, the tomorrows. Gone is the wonder of your life with me.

Child of my soul, now you belong to the ages; now you have transcended the boundaries of life and death.
You are no longer a child of this world,
but now and forever, you are a child of my soul.

Adolfo Quezada, a retired counselor and psychotherapist, has authored sixteen books on psycho-spiritual issues. He holds master's degrees in counseling and in journalism from the University of Arizona. Quezada is married and has four children and five grandchildren. He lives in Tucson, Arizona.